20 & Out

That's Your Bread and Butter?

Joel Arroyo

ISBN 13: 978-1981673070
ISBN 10: 1981673075

Dedication

To my loving Avi,

No matter the distance between us or how rare the days we share.

My love remains always and forever.

Foreword

There was no heat. No functional space heaters. All I had was an infant daughter without a clue of what was going on. I was broke. I mean broke.

No more money to get me over with credit cards. No cash in the bank. No check coming in for another two weeks. My accounts were in the negative and my pockets had just a few dollars left within their linty seams.

Worst part of it all, this was when I had a good paying job by most people's standards, with benefits and a pension plan.

I still recall my daughters face snuggled like an Eskimo, fixed with a smile, ready for more playtime, waving her itty-bitty limbs through the thick padding of fabrics I dressed her with, having no understanding of the struggle.

Money problems aside, I was at a low on all levels and my issue was much greater than I was. Working through the frustration, I paced around the house thinking of more solutions, finding brick wall after brick wall, stomping my feet. Not just for warmth, but at my failure as a man.

I had failed, unable to keep even the simplest of things—like warmth—provided to my newborn daughter.

With only so much overtime to go around and debts piling high, it was clear a change had to be made. In no way would the system change to accommodate my circumstance. So there was just one more option.

The change had to happen in me.

Table of Contents

Introduction

Unable to rest through all the noise in my head, I find myself in silence, sitting at the foot of the bed, staring at the reflection in the glass. The eyes staring back at mine look familiar, but I am afraid a perfect stranger would not appear much different.

The deep wrinkles stamped to his forehead, accenting those dark-pitted circles beneath his eyes, showed wear of years far beyond mine. The man in this mirror doesn't look like me at all. Even a smile appears to be a task for him. He looks exhausted.

After a moment's time, the man closes his eyes, sinks his head between his shoulders, bowing it to his chest like a child being scolded and shamed.

Eventually, his eyes rise and begin to follow the borders of the room, as if guided by a buzzing fly, only to, in the end, stare back into the glass with a look of total bewilderment.

I wonder why this man is not full of life when he appears to have it all. A job. A home. A car. Independence. What more could he want?

With a deep breath and a brief glance at the clock,

he drops his head one final time and reaches for the lamp string.

Lights out.

Can you relate to this scene? If you can, you are certainly not alone. In fact, according to several studies, like one conducted by The Harris Poll[1], only about one-third of people are 'very happy' with all areas in their life. So, what's up with the other sixty-seven percent?

The fact remains, most of us these days are only fully present in spurts and are never in one focused mental state long enough to truly identify with an in-depth understanding the direction we are headed.

Most would rather wait in the pauses of life, until the voices of their souls, coughing in the pollution, wake them. Even then, this awakening is just a momentary experience, a brief nightmare before going back to sleep.

After that, it is saved in the cloud as a memory and then onto another unfulfilling task. One thing is completed where another is delayed, allowing trivial things priority over discovering our unique identities and desires. Next thing you know, we are midway through life, in the middle of a dead end job with more mouths to

---

[1] http://www.theharrispoll.com/health-and-life/Annual_Happiness_Index_ Again_Finds_One-Third_of_Americans_Very_Happy.html

feed, having never lived a life of much substance at all.

Then we vary with ourselves, using all of our energy and resourcefulness on creating a sense of temporary progression. This cycle, while satisfying for the short term, always leads back to the need to refuel the illusion that things are moving forward.

We know this is not the formula for a fulfilling life. Still, we convince ourselves it is in the moment, until the nightmare haunts us all over again. Let's get real. We innately desire things to be long-lasting.

The unsaid truth is we can't take the idea that, perhaps just maybe, under our own watch, we could have settled for less. To absorb this concept without the proper mindset is what makes people crazy in their later years.

For this reason, we stay in a workplace or relationship that we already know like the back of our hand, no matter how stressful or dysfunctional it may be. We would rather live further from purpose *on purpose* than to be vulnerable to the potential pain we have chosen to associate with change.

If you apply what you're about to learn, you will be provided a fresh outlook that, by self-sacrifice, should more easily allow self-examination if this comes difficult. This could be what you have always needed to ignite that much-needed spark back into your life, as you know it.

All I ask is that you be selfish in these pages, and that you remain open-minded. For a moment, consider the fact that you have not arrived to "this" (chosen path) by mere chance. The objective isn't to change you, but to provide understanding on how you have arrived where you are today and to organically challenge whatever pillars you chose to accept as your identity.

I believe true freedom exists on the shoulders of men and women that live by using their gifts and talents without the need for approval. Others should only mirror or reinforce what you have already recognized as your path. To acknowledge your present condition and how far you may have strayed can only be brought to life through a disciplined daily self-examination. Consider those gifts you left behind miles ago.

Every experience—good or bad—shifts our gears according to degrees of influence impressed upon our individuality each time. These impressions, in turn, become stimuli forming areas of our mental construct. Forming what we perceive as our own identity.

In a moment's time, you can take on a mood and take on another in the next if you so deeply choose, so the choice to take on another's ways or outlook is purely adopted behavior. That said, it is when you can genuinely say with passion, "I do it all to myself by myself," that you will find this newfound drive to begin the rerouting process.

Don't worry if you can't come to grips with some of these concepts yet. The acceptance and application of such things, very much like our issues, do not just happen overnight. But we must also understand that anything CAN be changed overnight if this is what you truly desire.

Perhaps, you too have been renter of this pattern of life and have grown fond of this mirage, making habitual the nights of staring into the glass until the reflection is no more. Still uncertain?

Maybe a vicarious journey into the eyes of the man staring back at you is all you need to refocus and finally be the "you" that you always knew was there all along.

I am a grown man, with benefits and a pension plan. 20 Years & OUT. That's your bread and butter? But man can't live off bread alone. If even with butter for that matter.

Chapter 1: It All Comes Down to Perception

Here goes again. Half asleep and yawning after some much needed R&R. Still, the hours never seem to be enough.

I have awakened even moments before that sharp annoying tone of the alarm more times than can count. A part of me is thankful to have avoided at least that much this morning.

With a slow roll and a grunt only an old man could duplicate, my feet greet the cold, creaking wood beneath them. To no surprise, the neon digits on the clock have sprinted ahead. It is as if it possesses enough intelligence to spite me for my mandatory commute.

It's only Monday, yet Sunday is still napping as long as it desires. The voluntary framework pulls my every stride from the bedroom to the bathroom, to the kitchen, out the door, and into my vehicle, like clockwork.

Before buckling my seat belt, I look around to be sure no one is present, then check my holster to examine the extension of me. The safety must be off before I pull out of my driveway.

In one moment, everything can disappear for me. The home, the car, the things, and everything in between. In just a blink, someone else's perception could bring me to my ruin. My demise would be nothing but a casualty to one with an empty tank for rationale, and nobody would truly know the man beneath the stitching.

Have you ever taken the time to consider how influential, better yet, how limiting your perception can be? Perception plays a huge role in accessing your understanding in a moments time, especially when your life is on the line. It can easily be the difference between life and death.

Perception can assist us in identifying threatening situations or patterns of behavior. One's perception can be narrow, however, and trick us into believing what might be considered harm versus something that is not.

Let's consider an example to help you further understand why perception is so vital in your decision making. This alone can change your life if you let it.

Perhaps you are someone who has built a habit of talking on the phone while driving to work. Chances are, if you arrive at a red light and look across at another driver moving their lips inside their vehicle, you would probably assume they were on a Bluetooth. This could trigger you to call someone after processing this thought.

On the other hand, let's suppose you usually choose to listen to music on your commute and enjoy having a "lip-syncing extravaganza." In this respect, the other driver would more likely appear to be living a moment from your lens of life, listening to music and singing themselves.

This simple scenario serves as a prime example of how our perceptions each day give way to guiding our thoughts. Hence, when you consider this truth, you begin to realize that the mental lens is only as strong as the individual behind the wheel.

In other words, if you have a security-driven scope of things, you will begin to create a world revolving around that axis of thought. This perception will take over all others.

If this is true, then recognizing this must also allow us the same ability to reconsider the way we view ourselves, which, in turn, must also allow us the ability to modify the reality in which we live.

Of course, we go through experiences which influence perception as well. But once you are aware of your common perceptions—the way you look at things and identify what it is attached to—you can then change your world in ways you may have never thought of before. So, instead of seeing things in one limited perception, let us take this time now to consider others.

Go back to the example of your commute and seeing the other driver's lips move and fix your mind to accept other possibilities of what might be happening. Create more options that were not there before. With one hypothesis, it may be possible that you are correct, but the more options that are given to each scenario can only improve your chances of having the correct answer with increased certainty.

For instance, the individual in the other vehicle could have been learning how to speak a language or maybe he or she was recanting an audio book. This simple exercise allows us to understand more thoroughly the power of perception and how it can help install new ways of thought when we use it.

But this can only be achieved by taking the time to notice when we are acting in a narrow-minded manner. If we refuse to lend our minds to other possible options, the chances of opening ourselves up to more freeing choices within our unfulfilling cycle only grows in its limitations.

Another good example to further relate this is to consider the subject of eyewitness testimony in criminal cases. This brand of testimony is only taken with a grain of salt. Do you know why that is? Because one's perception can easily skew the real details of what occurred since the only reality that exists in us is the one we create.

Have you ever spoken to someone who has worked in a specific occupation for a long period of time and asked them a question outside of their chosen field? They have a tendency to use the parameters they have practiced in so much that their thought process compliments it. Their limited scope is a benefit on the job, but not with everything else.

Don't get me wrong, there are many things that go into our decision making. But perception is a huge driver in directing the same pattern of thought behavior. Therefore, it becomes a huge determinant of our direction.

Couple that perception with a strong belief and the story we tell ourselves becomes nearly impossible to change. In this case, you would have a hard time telling someone they did not see what they are convinced they saw.

Similarly, if we decide to produce excuses or flag things as having higher priority over others, further backing those excuses with strong enough belief, I assure you that, without a shift, you will be left in the same idling fulfillment.

How long have you been lending yourself out to others like a book on a shelf, going from job to job, leaving personal fulfillment behind? The first thing is to replace this pattern with a new belief where you view your time as worthwhile and limited.

Most of us don't do a thing about our own fulfillment because we either don't know how or tell ourselves some other excuse that fills in the gap of truth for a while. That is, until we grow sick of what we do or become depressed from doing the same thing for so long without anything to show for ourselves.

Do you think life is still too busy to invest in yourself? Lend your mind for a moment to your everyday commute and let's discuss what I like to call "attention profiting" or "chauffeured profiting."

While we remain in a trance, driving our vehicles to our usual destinations, others are using their time to create more value for themselves. We know this because we see them, but do we really consider our own value in the mix?

Observe the advertisements posted alongside the highway, vying for just a moment of our attention to plant a seed of branding. How about the man dressed up as a pizza, waving the sign for a new deal as your stomach gurgles and your mouth salivates?

Radio stations turn to commercial breaks, with yet another giveaway or sponsored product, to feel the pulse of who is listening in, all to make their station the one with most value. Ding! Your GPS sends you nearby suggestions that you never even asked it to provide.

Your mind and time is always bombarded, trying to be filled and used up by everything else everywhere, and they don't seem to have a problem with it. The key here is to realize that these things would not exist if there weren't people available to provide value to their efforts.

So your time—while not perceived as much value to you for one reason or another—definitely proves important to the rest. Still don't have time?

Do not be fooled; money can be earned and spent, but data feeds on itself with compounding interest. Using nothing but our sweet time we: listen to the radio, watch television, interact with online media, and spend time on many other avenues of "chauffeured profiting" today.

Please don't misconstrue the idea I am attempting

to bring home here. The concept of spending time wisely should be examined carefully. Being aware with how we use our time is vital because it directs our minds.

If you hear something enough, you begin to believe it. If you see something enough, you begin to remember it. If you believe something enough, you begin to speak it. Who knows what else could result in your life with this realization.

Chapter 2: And Then There Is Me

VROOOOOOOOOMMMMMM...

My attention escapes from the driver beside me to the light turning green, permitting me to continue the commute as usual. Every facet of me drips away like the rain on my windshield.

The half-hour travel builds with gradually increasing anxiety, proving a necessary tool for my survival once again.

"So you train; you shall fight," the physical training instructors would always say, a stern reminder to remain on high alert no matter how comfortable the audience makes you feel. After all, anybody could decide it will be a bloody day if the wind blew the wrong direction.

Hell, I have witnessed a bad visit alone take a

calm eight-hour shift to a mandated sixteen-hour extraction fest, full of floods and feces gliding along cell floors.

Just some long-lasting sweaty population management, the reward of which is another opportunity to punch out and follow the same framework the following day. Hoorah!

Savoring these last moments of total silence, I take inventory and begin going over all of the "what if" situations in my head as preparation for what might be waiting for me inside the walls.

With a diverse population and odds stacked against me, every day is bound to present something different from the next. And with a measly four hours of sleep in order to arrive on time, sound judgment is a task in and of itself.

A study carried out by A.M. Williamson and Anne – Marie Feyer states, "commonly experienced sleep deprivation depressed performance to a level equivalent to that produced by alcohol intoxication of at least a BAC of 0.05%. At the end of periods of waking of 17-19 hours, performance levels were low enough to be accepted in many countries as incompatible with safe driving.[2]" This

---

[2] https://www.ncbi.nlm.nih.gov/pmc/articles/PMC1739867/

means that a lack of rest followed by remaining up for at least seventeen hours and you may as well call an Uber to return to work.

A couple of ramps, a few lights, and the big blue sign is on my left. I'm just three speed bumps away from the lot now. I can already see barbed wire in the distance as an oncoming vehicle whizzes by, throwing a hard breeze at my door.

Pulling into a spot in the main parking area, it all appears so desolate. But, rest assured, the belly of the beast inside roars like a few missed meals, nothing but hatred eating away at it.

One last glance at the sky's tears and three clips fasten my belt for the real ride. But this ride lasts for more than a half an hour. Might mean back-to-back sixteen hour days if enough individuals with more seniority call it quits and call out, a tactic commonly used to convince themselves they possess at least some control in it all, only to find, at some point, they must once again return.

The emotions on the surface display laughter in their drunken slumbers, but they too must pay the beast for a chance to get away once more. Some do their best to get by and find the time worked each week as a fair trade. Others fall short and get walked out for resorting to diluted strategies in search of a quick fix to make for a faster retirement.

After retirement, many are thankful, deciding to tilt the glass to appear more full. Most believe hard, manual, unfulfilling labor is a necessary step to living like a king later, when it's all over.

*Then, of course, there is **me**.*

Chapter 3: Hindsight is 20/20

> "Failure is the opportunity to live again more intelligently."
>
> ~ Henry Ford

I am going to give twenty years to live for twenty years. Sounds like a good plan, right? It is if, statistically, I surpass the average life expectancy of those who came before me in this line of work. If all of the promises are provided after these twenty years, I will make bank!

It's been so long I have forgotten what it was that sparked the interest to live this ecstatic visualization all the way to the achievement. What gave me so much energy to go through it all and end with the highest scores in the whole 242 Alpha Arsenals class, for that matter?

Piss and vinegar maybe. I was just this young man in training, rerunning scores of the Rocky soundtrack in my head to keep me pushing. This physically fit, lean, mean, spiritual machine.

Regardless of how pumped my muscles could ever become, my mind could never fully prepare for something like this until years down the line.

I have this cartoonlike image now, as if the whole process of reaching retirement is like a long-awaited bus stop. Everyone gives a handshake and finds a seat before squinting their eyes, sorting through the foggy distance, all in unison, in search of a silhouette. But for most of the years, it's only a carrot.

When it does arrive, they are either a tombstone, in a wheelchair, or nearly have a heart attack when they find their seat. Just a long-awaited bus stop, looking for those green sliding letters of "bread and butter."

This is when the image peels away like a film screen transition, revealing some snazzy salesman behind the scenes, like the small man in the Wizard of Oz, stating the following:

> *"For these twenty years, you will not just have the pension, but be fully vested medically for the rest of your life and until your children are 26 years old. Not to mention, the constant potential to be sued, knocked out of raises for ten or more of those years, be violently assaulted, possibly killed, and exposed to all diseases including MRSA, HIV, TB, and the works. Each day you step foot in this wonderful place blowing air ventilation to share with*

all that breathes within it. Life expectancy for those in this occupation is 58 years old, so you'd better think fast because every day counts! Wait...there's more! You get free socks and complimentary work boots every six months, at least this year, depending on the Union standing since you'll be needing those on your feet and all. And don't forget: If the future is promising, as a thanks, every year you give past your twenty years we will tack on 2% to your annual salary. So, reach for the stars and remember: You are appreciated."

To stomach all of this at once and keep going back for seconds (and thirds) might sound stupid. But without someone to eat the meals in the first place, how would anyone ever know its effects?

Besides, the risk portion seems to slip away when there's a gym full of hundreds of men and women standing beside you, ready to do the same. My infatuation with the thrill of standing out in the crowd, as one of the elite, didn't make risk much a focus either. And the potential to make more than anyone in my family had ever earned made it insatiable. What!?!

Do you think those exposures would be enough for you to say no? They always say hindsight is 20/20. The real effects can't be felt until you're in the thick of it.

In one informative article by Gary G. Felt, *The Relationship of Post-Traumatic Stress Disorder to Law Enforcement: The Importance of Education*, he states:

"Because a law enforcement career usually lasts for at least twenty years, the duration criterion is met. Clinically significant distress or impairment in social, occupational, or other important areas of functioning all too often show up in an officer's life as evidenced by high divorce, alcoholism, and suicide rates…When it comes to PTSD, individuals going into law enforcement do so with the deck stacked against them from the start! It is a natural 'set up' for PTSD or other stress-related diseases and maladies.[3]"

---

[3] http://www.aaets.org/article92.htm

Chapter 4: The Downward Spiral

> "When someone is falling, the tendency is to get on a downward spiral that can eventually become a self-fulfilling prophecy."
>
> ~ Tony Robbins

The taste was more than I could bear now, so the sting of strong drinking took the edge off. And with the drinking came plenty more. Let's just say a lifestyle of bottomless desires to temporarily ease the pressure was the habit.

To push ahead and elevate, using a slew of demeaning routines, trying to fill the void where hope and excitement joined, added to the blindness. I was drowning in the depths of destruction with dwindling aspirations.

Upon entrance, I was an ordained Youth Pastor who had assigned himself to this warzone. I was a prayer warrior ready to take on anything, and then, within just a few years, I would find divorce by an unfaithful wife, later yet finding a baby out of wedlock.

The downward spiral continued. At this point, the taste may as well have been tested with a blindfold, because it all tasted bitter.

Just political mumbo jumbo and once again no raises. The gossipers had more to gossip about, brownnosers had another conversation-starter with the higher ups while brewing their morning coffee, and us workers went on without a hitch. The more senior staff would just use a comparative example of how it happened to them, as though it was another notch on the belt.

What always amazed me was how much was taken away, yet how much the work would stay the same or increase in demand. It's even more amazing how far from your purpose you can go when your legs feel anchored to the buffed floors, awaiting benefits for a future that may never arrive.

In this capsule of time, I looked beyond myself, revealing the truth that would set in stone the real meaning of freedom, to me, forever.

This brings me to the core of why any words meet paper at all, to find your eyes living through mine for a moment in time. But don't read on if you're not ready. It may not be an easy bite to take, let alone a full meal once it is served.

Chapter 5: The Revelation

It's quite brisk as I take pulls from my cigarette, admiring the moonlit sky, a cheap thermal to block the wind chill. In this moment of finding fresh air a luxury, I am reminded of the thought that, in just another 15 years, I should be free to do exactly what I want, when I want, in the very fashion I choose.

A usual struggle of mine would be to justify. This would come so easy to me after a while. I would say, "Well, most people never have the chance to retire in their 40s with the potential to make forty grand a year indefinitely." It was almost as if justification and weighing the pros and cons were the only way to find hope for day-by-day survival.

The air reveals its chill as the last pull just shy of the filter escapes my cold lips. It was only at the end of this, and in the process of going back into the warmth of my one-bedroom apartment, that my gaze fell from the moon to this small tree before me.

In this tree, I observe a nest, not occupied of course, due to the cold-hitting winter in Connecticut. It had few leaves remaining on its limbs, exposing its roots just above the dead patches of surrounding grass.

I could not speak, but only stare at this tree in awe at its bare, natural beauty, thinking only of what it meant to me in this moment.

This wasn't the first time I had come out to enjoy a smoke. Yet, with paralyzed eyes on this nest that rested between the two strongest limbs down to its roots, I came to a relevant conclusion.

There are just two types of people in this world: Those who choose to be the root and those who choose to remain in the nest.

The whole time, I had been so focused on the goal of living a life of freedom, only to find myself more entrenched in what I had dug. I had been digging myself into the ground just as the roots of this tree dug so deep that it spread twice as large as its trunk.

Since my youth, I had always pushed for more than my predecessors, which was a low standard to begin with, so anything honest was a start really.

Being the younger of two siblings, I had to settle for public school, food stamps, and plenty hand-me-downs, but it didn't matter. Fact is, I had settled and chose to act as if, by reaching a bit further than the set standard in my family, I had reached the pinnacle of my existence. Like now I could live it out a few pegs higher and appreciate that I had made it.

"What a croc!" I thought, still mentally marinating with dropped jaw at something as simple as this tree outside my apartment complex.

I remembered my father telling me something after shaking a few hands following the close of the graduating ceremony. He said he had always wanted to be what I had become, which begged the question of whether his unattained desire reinforced my emotions, further empowering my false sense of accomplishment and pride.

Not many children get to hear these words from someone who brought them into this world. Apparently it meant enough to me to stay on this track and persevere even more.

With this momentum, the fact remained, although I couldn't tell at the time, the difference between those who decide to be the roots versus those who decide to nest lies in whether they are willing to relentlessly ignore the battle.

Without recalibrating throughout each day, the road can easily become a highway to somewhere totally unintended. Remember: there are perceptions and beliefs, and then there are our moods and emotions that serve as avenues for reinforcing or redirecting our mental compasses.

With enough ignorance and time, one can totally snuff out a higher-purpose mentality by recanting internal and external self-imposed limitations in every avenue of communication. This leads to a life full of self-degradation by default.

How do I know? Because, I willingly chose this route. I thought that by rearranging the emotions I had attached to my occupation, it would give me the oomph needed to make me enjoy it. It didn't.

It began taking more energy to be something I was not while neglecting the cultivation of those things I was, just not in the physical yet. How far had I strayed?

Chapter 6: Stepping Back

<blockquote>

"The meaning of life is whatever you ascribe it to be."

~ Joseph Campbell

</blockquote>

I was about twelve years old and my uncle was babysitting me as he or one of my mother's close friends usually would when she decided to go out partying or whatever the excused absence.

Probably an attempt to pay herself back for the time she had lost caring for two children by herself best she could, or maybe to mask the pains of lost love. Anyway, little did I know, this night would be one to be remembered and change my life forever.

BOOM!

The door flings open and I hear nothing but "FREEEEEZE!!!" as this silhouette of a giant put a cold to my forehead and a beam of light in my eyes.

Seated near the television, I held my bowl of cereal, spoonful still in my mouth. The same treatment was received by my uncle as he shrieked in terror, awakened from a deep sleep on the couch adjacent to mine.

"Get up" and "Sit down" they said sternly. My uncle got up and I followed suit, sitting at the dining room table, a few steps from the couch, in total compliance.

I recall not feeling fear, though shock at first, followed by confusion. This place was supposed to be safe and quiet unless the noise was produced by those within.

Once out of the daze, I became a sponge taking in all my eyes could absorb from the man questioning my uncle like those men I had only seen on television shows. Others inside were tossing, opening, and slamming cabinet drawer after cabinet drawer in the kitchen, even poking through the fridge for anything out of sorts, while another in the group began flipping the mattress and box spring in my mother's bedroom.

Distant banging in what had to be the bathroom echoed while every couch was removed of its cushions, cluttering wherever they landed.

This is when one officer asked me to show him my bedroom, so I did. I wondered if he would be the one to flip my mattress and toss my things about while I just watch, a spectator of what was once an organized safe-haven to escape to whenever life felt too loud.

Following him, I walked into my room and sat on the bed. While looking around, he began asking general questions like how I was doing in school and what grade I was in.

He then stopped and asked about the four-tiered shelf displaying mixed achievements from school and sports with trophies, plaques, and ribbons dressing it perfectly. It was at this point that the officer complimented the tidiness of the room and decided not to touch anything in it. Being such a neat freak since I was very young, the room was always in order and everything had its place.

Maybe his decision was one of respect and appreciation for two children doing so well, though my brother would hardly stay with us since, most nights, he found refuge at grandma's house. It was then the man said, "You're going to be very successful someday, as long as you stay on the path you're on."

Now, we all know that success is more of a relative term but, at that age, I was just thankful to have received such a compliment from anyone. Being an introvert, no words escaped my mouth.

The focus, however, is not of the circumstance or my lack of father-bonding, but rather the correlation that I formulated, deeming law as good. A man of the law stating well done, thus far, must've meant a lot.

Listen, I was just a kid, but I knew enough to know this wasn't just some mistake. I lived around drugs, money, and sex prematurely. And even though most adults—including my own mother—would try to hide things in speech or brush a hand when I walked in a room unannounced, I was hip to more than most children my age.

But we had to live, so I knew, especially after watching so much COPS, this is what happens, which sends me back to where becoming one of the law became my goal. Through grade school I had been safety patrol and the president of the student council, walking in the steps of the law in the minutest of ways as a child.

If only I could step back in time and see that man today. Would he say after reading this that he was a root? Or would he favor the nest?

Either way, my well-intentioned but misdirected desire to be something of worth was only translated into useful energy thrown in a direction that yielded success by most individual's standards, except for the *most important person*…the one living the achievement.

All of this proved certain that, no matter what it is I want, I can have or become. I could have wanted to be the next movie star, and so long as I desired to, I would have been.

See, even the road to hell is paved with good intentions but, without a plan to follow and a complete understanding of your footing, one can only expect the same outcome.

What is influencing *you* today? Is it fear or a desire to live by the standards of others? Perhaps it is simply the lack of understanding of yourself that caused your path to become a winding road?

It is only in understanding yourself more that you can pair your life with what is fulfilling for you. Let's make things clearer for you.

Chapter 7: Taking Risks

"If it's still in your mind, it is worth taking the risk."

~ Paul Coelho

Where are the birds now that built and occupied this nest, to live for a time in this branch? Better yet, what gave them the desire to fly, though staying put was always an option, even if it did mean a struggle until reaching spring, much like a bus after twenty?

While nests are generally used for eggs and hatching, to keep away from predators in this instance, it's a reminder of a place where its occupants left, no matter how warm or how comfortable it may have been for a time.

Did you know that a bird's body is programmed to migrate when the weather gets cold? The only difference between them and us, of course, is in how much we choose to listen to our bodies.

Have you ever entered into your workplace and felt a weight on your back the closer you got to the door? How about tightness in your chest with mental anxiety accompanying it?

See, it is one thing to possess the ability to "migrate," but another to possess the gift, talent, or desire to reach toward fulfillment and never take the risk since what we can lose appears more important than what we can gain. This essentially is the great divide between those who choose to be roots and those who choose to nest.

Before I left, I informally interviewed several coworkers in the breakroom or in passing. To no surprise, they revealed the *real* sacrifice, the one even the most persevered suffered from.

> **Co-worker A** – "I went to school and obtained a degree and, if I had the chance to do it all over again, I would have taught and done what made me happy and made me feel rewarded. I have two kids, so that's it for me. But I would say to you, never lose your dream. Follow your dreams because, in the end, that's all that matters."

> **Co-worker B** – "I want to pay my bills, but I just can't get myself to come to work for overtime. In fact, I spend more money to fill my void and find myself more depressed, so I use up all the days off that I

have. I just can't get a break."

Co-worker C – "If I could do it all over again, I would have done something else because, to tell you the truth, I feel like I wasted time here. And even though I have a pension when I retire, in a few months at this point, I don't feel like I have done much with my life worth noting."

The intention isn't to downgrade this occupation, but to shed light on the real impact one word can have on our destiny: risk.

Risk is usually a word synonymous with pain and fear, having negative associations with the outcome of taking it. So, ultimately, instead of harnessing our true potential and looking beyond the risk towards the result, we remain spectators in our own world, living below the means of what our true potential contains.

Not to mention, in most, if not all interviews, the mental inability to leave most times was attached to something dealing with finances and time invested. The truth is, the longer you remain where you are, the longer you will probably stay in that occupation, whether you enjoy it or not.

Isn't this the law of inertia? Well, consider this act

of risk on my behalf, exposing my experiences and journey, as the action to put everything in motion for *your* life. It takes nothing but one change today to shift the whole world in your favor tomorrow.

Don't create this justified rationale, ultimately landing you in the same ditch, not taking strides toward a new world or a new venture. How many people do you know use such justification to determine this path of least resistance? I could picture myself driving to work every day doing just that. But not anymore!

I knew I needed to get pushing and use my mind as a tool to get me out of this place, if I ever had the guts. So I began reading and listening to audio books, watching educational videos, and doing my best to apply at least one thing a day.

I would read everything I could get my hands on that dealt with self-help or how people thought and behaved. I figured I was going to work smarter and not harder. People kept pumping the iron, I kept cracking the spines. Others kept drinking, I kept pouring on the knowledge.

I would take notes from every book I read and focus only on those things that benefitted me. It was the only way I would escape the mental prison I had created in my mind.

Nobody else cared enough to pay me what I was worth, so I decided to set up a mental savings account that would gain interest over the years. When I needed to lower my debt, I turned to Dave Ramsey. When I needed outlooks or financial advice, I would study Robert Kiyosaki's books and keep my eyes on his 'Rich Dad.'

I came across other names like Zig Ziglar, Jim Rohn, Tony Robbins, Les Brown, and the list only grew. Something was being installed inside me that I never knew was possible.

My outlook was shifting.

Chapter 8: Creating Discipline

> "Discipline is the bridge between goals and accomplishment."
>
> ~ Jim Rohn

Each day, before bedtime, I would find myself at the foot of my bed, internally asking myself questions focused only on what I loved to do. I would sit, eyes closed, and live in a moment that used my talents and gifts.

In my case, it was visualizing myself speaking to massive groups of people, expounding upon the various steps and ways we can meet in total empowerment.

In this deep seated position, my hands would become sweaty, my heart would race, and the sounds of the crowd would become clear as day. It was to the point that, every night I did this, I no longer needed to close my eyes so see it.

This habit became so disciplined that it was hard for me to remain seated, so I stood up. I soon found myself pacing in the space and eventually speaking aloud, as though the crowd were really before me.

This routine became so anchored that every conversation would be left with evidence of the fact that this was my destiny and purpose.

See, the beauty of it all is that, when you believe to such a degree that you can see it clearly, nobody can tell you otherwise. When you believe with such conviction, no naysayer can change the direction.

Do as I did now. Find a quiet place and take a seat. And don't just sit down and see yourself. Focus on one thing at a time.

First, focus on the sounds associated with the image you have chosen, the one that displays your action. Get associated with the physical feelings, down to the taste of the saliva in your mouth.

What are you wearing? What are you doing, exactly? Are you painting the most amazing piece of art? Yes? What shades did you decide on and what size is the picture frame you surrounded your art in?

Be specific. The more you add to the image, the more it will come alive. An easy way to remember this step is to do what I call "dressing the mannequin."

Visualize each article of clothing being placed onto a mannequin. This is usually easier because mannequins arrive in our minds, many times without heads or just some legs to put just a few items on before they are complete. This is an especially good routine if you're a designer at heart.

If you are a speaker, what emotion can you feel? Focus on the setting to the degree that the smell of the presenter's cologne or perfume handing you the microphone is present as well.

If you are a hair dresser, feel the shears in your hand as you hold the client's hair in the other. Where are you? Is it a salon or a place of your own?

If you're studying to be a surgeon, instead of just reading the words and memorizing, see yourself creating new ways to improve the future of the world through your precision and creativity. We are only as weak as the image we involve ourselves in. If you see yourself, you will finally be yourself.

It is evenly important to keep in mind that not every day will be a good day through the process. Expect some days to be harder than others, but never neglect the discipline.

The routine will be harder to break the longer you do it. Soon you will be doing it without even realizing it because the life you saw for yourself and the one you lead will become the same.

Chapter 9: Developing Courage

> "Success is not final, failure is not fatal. It is the courage to continue that counts."
>
> ~ Winston Churchill

Months went by and each one was that much more unfulfilling as my mind went through the nightly mantra.

My thoughts went from, "How could I make this work?" to the even bigger question, "What will it take for me to leave this month?"

Even though I could visualize and see myself in this arena, and the image was clearer than ever, I still had to make the real decision. I had to leave what I had known for seven years, day in and day out. What I had prepared for my entire life.

One thing to remember is that, no matter how much we can see it, we have to take the step to show that it's more than just a dream. Otherwise that *is* all it is, just a dream.

This newfound awareness, however, helped

muster some momentum as every moment that I didn't utilize my gifts would deliver this unsettling feeling underneath my hardened shell which began to fill my cup of courage more and more.

Conversations were chock full of these jewels of confirmation that I was on to something freeing this time around. Those old small talk phrases like, "This is the life huh?" didn't resonate with me any longer.

The obvious prolonged stares became welcome mats for me to further my intentions. Most would look at me as this dreamer, as if the ability to leave didn't exist or didn't make sense. Why would it!?! It will be you changing in an unchanging world.

Interestingly, the staff I did speak to who still had a while before their uniform would show the wear of their years were all ears. Maybe because the place hadn't settled on them yet. Nonetheless, there had only been a handful of people who decided to leave on their own and move onto something else.

Understandably, what I was setting the sails to do was found taboo. If the previous who had the desire didn't die before their time in the line of duty or due to drugs or health conditions, many died just days or a few years beyond receiving their pension and never had the chance.

To make matters worse, many got other jobs to assist their finances after retirement. Can you imagine doing something you never enjoyed for 20 years and still having a need for a small part-time job to make due, or to fill in time after habitually working 16 hour shifts back-to-back?

I finally got sick and tired of being sick and tired, of being just a body assimilating, having no individuality or purpose but to run into situations most usually run from. I became fixated on the facts, keeping in mind my lower-middle class standing, despite the caliber of man waiting to burst out of the seams in my mind.

It's ironic how the history of Hitler and his attempt to rule through genocide resonated somehow. Not literally by any means but, rather, in relation to the idea that we had all become slaves. Lured with a carrot, we could only receive by becoming one big gang, identified with a badge on a shirt and a last name above the pen in a pocket.

How could I have found myself here without any expression of self, unable to even crack a window for fresh air or make a call to check in with the outside world? The entry to these places isn't like a smile welcoming you with some coffee. Instead, it's a rush to the entry door, responding to a code called to reduce the chances of an assault becoming any worse or to separate multiple attackers.

Welcome home to the brickyard. Here you check your bags in *after* they're scanned by a fellow supervisory officer you hope didn't have a chip on his or her shoulder, keeping you at the door longer than necessary.

After, several doors slam behind you and awaken every fiber you thought might have still been at rest, your access is gained only by another member of the gang hopefully being alert on the other end of the camera. Especially since these posts are commonly held by those who decide to do a few years over twenty.

Don't get me wrong, many of these staff members were wise and very much on the ball when reacting to an incident. But, when you have seen complacency leave an officer down or leave *you* battling with two at once, you begin to understand that you are on your own…up until you aren't.

Don't let someone on light duty find a way into the brain of control because, those days, you are nothing but a mouse in a maze. No fault to the system. The fault belonged to me.

What helped me finally rid myself of excuses and take that leap of risk was probably what you can relate to or will be able to relate to someday. I thought only of my daughter. She was only one or two at the time, when this decision seemed most pressing.

Do I stay here and end up just as those interviewed coworkers, unfulfilled and nothing noteworthy to live towards but a pension? Or do I make a move most only wish to have the guts to do and build my own life by creating a fulfilling system?

Ironically, while working in the prison system, the family court system deemed that, even after a fight for more time, six days a month with my daughter was enough. One system to another had a flaw. What I did had no weight. I was just another father in Connecticut.

I hated not having time with her, not having enough money to give her things without sacrificing more of what I didn't have enough of. Time.

Before coming to the decision of leaving, I recall forfeiting my mind to others at times, even if not in the physical form. I would think of people I looked up to or coworkers with seniority, rolling their eyes, convinced I was some selfish-minded man too fragile for real life.

Surely, they must be right? Who, as a parent, shouldn't be pleased to teach their child to always be themselves and bring to the world your gifts without compromise? When you look in the eyes of the most fragile life and hold it in your hands, you should be able to tell them more than to work hard for someone else.

My internal dialogue would go back and forth some days. In time, I came to the conclusion that my life was mine to live and the ideologies of others were formed some place too just, not where mine lived.

Certainly, I could have weighed my options on the outlook of many more individuals and on the concept of what work was to them. Instead, I asked how *I* felt this time around. Especially after taking note of how many people lived my life for me those past seven years.

I figured, if I was going to be broke from a lack of change in circumstance—after "making a voluntary move to change my career" as the child court so eloquently stated—while working in this always-changing system, taking and giving back raises, constantly laying off and hiring again, back-to-back 16-hour shifts without rest while placing my life on the line each day, and *still* suffer later on from the effects, what would I have to lose? PTSD? Ha-ha.

Hell, I was already mentally noting every exit upon entrance to every fast food place. I was the guy sitting with my back to the wall, wearing two pieces, sometimes considering myself a target because, many times, I was by default.

One story after the next would find its way into the cold walls. Every news bulletin of this week's officer assaulted, maimed, or killed; found after trying to pump some gas or buy his child something at the nearest convenience store. Some life, huh? Nothing to lose in hindsight.

It wasn't so easy. But with a different mental construct, it could have easily been the reason to remain caught up in the rat race, too fearful of making a move in any direction.

Already pressed on both sides, it was no easy task, but I imagined, when my daughter was grown, what would I want of *her* to become? Filled with purpose, or in the oars of another's ship because of what the rest of the world thought?

Using this drive and rationale as daily reinforcement eventually pushed me over the edge from, "Maybe I should?" to "Sir, here…my two weeks' notice." I had finally done it.

The cup of courage was filled to the brim.

Chapter 10: The Mental Briefcase

Okay now, first thing is first. In order for *you* to fully experience through my eyes the full effect of this ultimate eye-opening journey, you must first be true to yourself this time around.

This revelation was not provided to me in some magical way. It is definitely not an advertisement for smoking either, just in case that has entered your minds.

This moment was an inevitable result based on the foundation that was set in place. In order to get to this point, however, it was vital to move things around like a Rubik's Cube in my mind, regardless of my outward present state.

To give a better understanding of what I mean, follow me through a few brief exercises as this simple moment can do the same for you if you're up for it. Either way, it will reinforce your direction or, for the first time, gauge your life on a page to finally embark on a journey you have always desired.

Best of all, these take less time to complete than it does to pay the bills, so I encourage you to take this opportunity and invest moments now to save you years of discontentment and regret down the line.

Exercise 1

If you are even remotely familiar with or have read anything geared toward self-help, your 'why' is probably something you have grown tired of hearing about.

But the fact is, without it, your subconscious will never be able to solidify the true direction you want to keep pushing towards. Instead, it will throw around a few ideas to fulfill a few directions, depending on whatever seems a pressing priority in moments, which will ultimately leave you swimming in circles.

If you apply these moments in the most focused state, this will make certain that there is constantly one main drive toward your success, whatever that may be. In my case, it was fulfillment and a chance to use my gifts and talents for the betterment of others.

But, enough about me. If you would allow me, free-write on a sheet of paper--without stopping for one full minute—to get *your* 'why's' out.

> **Example:** Freedom to do what I love to do all the time. A chance to display my passion, intelligence, creativity, and inspire the world by my life experiences. To tell my story through my eyes, with my emotions and my views and feelings. Because I am sick of working for other people without making a living and, instead, making other people richer. Because I am worth more than money and, as a father, my legacy is paramount.

Everything you have ever believed might scare you because your excuses are going to show. So, if you have been bullshitting yourself all this time, you, my friend, are in for a treat.

Exercise 2

Once the last exercise is complete, you also want to write down all the reasons you have not arrived to your destination…yet.

If you have already arrived at your desired destination, use this opportunity to reinforce your reasons as it can only empower you more and potentially wipe out any lingering mental detours down the road.

I personally never had the privilege of knowing off the bat. I dreaded the question of "What do you want to be?" in high school. Having no clue, I was destined for some wasted energy. Anyhow, this is where, just by looking at my list as an adult, I became a little pissed off to say the least.

But I don't want to guide your answers with my personal summary. Instead, see the example below and jot down *your* personal reasons, again for one full minute without stopping, and see what reasons you find.

> **Example:** Because I fear of losing whatever income I do have. Fear of not being able to pay my bills. Fear of failure and being even worse off than I am now. Not enough time to begin with. I am consumed with work. Laziness. The time I have I would rather catch up on sleep.

Exercise 3

Ultimately, this last exercise is what ties it all together. Once you have an idea as to why you desire a more promising outcome than the one you decided to settle into, you get the chance to see your excuses for what they really are.

The only thing left to do is get real about what you

want and ask yourself how bad you want it. So, same as previously, jot down all of your reasons. Feel free to use the example to better understand what is required here.

> **Example:** I have been through so much in my life, I feel like I deserve to be well-off and successful. I want to be able to travel wherever, whenever I want. I want to stand for independence and conquering fears to accomplish a dream most people fear and waste too much time worrying to ever become. I want to make my daughter proud and give her what I didn't have. I want to be able to spend more time with her in her most important and active years of her life. I want to be that seed of inspiration to everyone who has ever lived a life of constant worry and anxiety.

Review the reasons that required the least thought. Those are the ones that were written with passion behind them. Circle them in red to remind you that these desires are deeply imbedded in your heart. Then, for each of those circled in red, take a moment and visualize yourself feeling as though you have accomplished these desires already, one by one. This will help you connect each desire that much deeper.

How does it feel? What do you see? How do you see others looking at your life now? If closing your eyes through this process helps, then do so.

Take 30 seconds to visualize accomplishing each one individually. Time begins NOW!

CONGRATULATIONS!!!

First and foremost, I commend you on taking the time out for yourself to complete these exercises. The best part is that you now have a reference sheet that will be nothing short of life changing.

Keep this someplace visible, like on your bathroom mirror, for instance. Hell, make a few copies and spoil yourself with reinforcement each morning and each night before you go to bed to remind yourself and hold yourself accountable.

If you really want something better, this is how you start.

Conclusion

"The only thing worse than being blind is having sight but no
vision."
~ Hellen Keller

After reading this, you should have a very good understanding of who you are and what events have brought you to this point in your life.

The question is, what are you going to do with this new perspective?

I made plenty of wrong turns along the way to ultimately get me to where I am today. Unfortunately, I delayed things for a good while because of them. I decided to let the opinions of others determine my direction in life. This book was created to be a voice for everyone willing to use my experiences so they do not have to do the same.

But, I can't put a stop to your limiting beliefs. I can only encourage you to come away from the shadows of your limiting thoughts and reveal yourself for the world to see. Someone is counting on you to become yourself so that they can become themselves. That is just the way it works. Inspiration is an amazingly powerful tool but passion is what breaks habits and changes lives.

There is something that happens in that journey of self-discovery that no book could ever quite explain. You are going to have to experience that for yourself. But, the only way to create this journey is to demonstrate it.

So, I dare you to be more than a skeptic of your own story. I dare you to finally open your eyes and see the truth. Your path is more significant than a cushy job can ever offer.

Remember, it is not about feeding the tummies of our children or those with less. Making a real impact means to feed others in ways that will never allow them to starve in your absence.